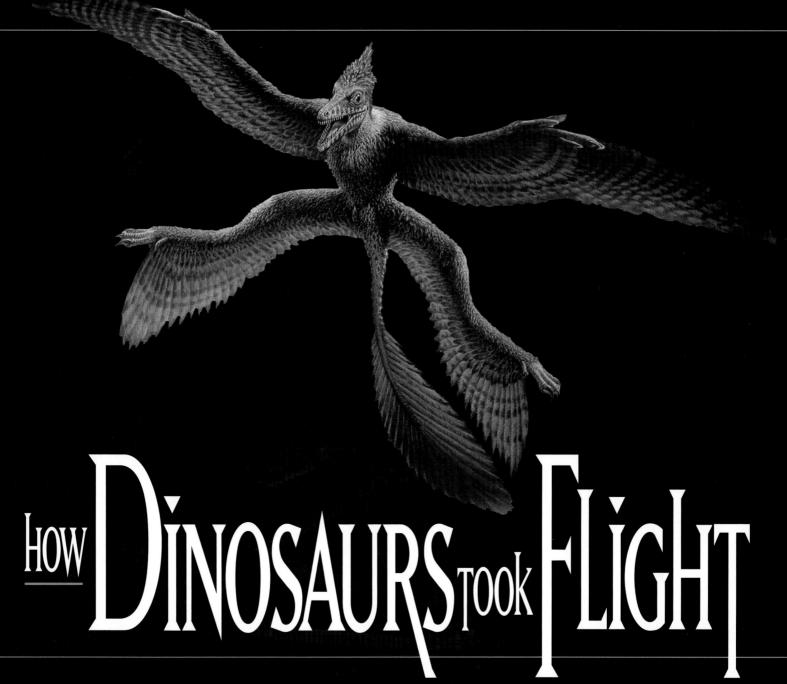

HOW DINOSAURS TOOK FLIGHT

THE FOSSILS, THE SCIENCE, WHAT WE THINK WE KNOW, AND THE MYSTERIES YET UNSOLVED

Christopher Sloan
Foreword by Dr. Xu Xing

NATIONAL GEOGRAPHIC
Washington, D.C.

Published by the National
Geographic Society
1145 17th St. N.W.
Washington, D.C. 20036-4688

John M. Fahey, Jr.
*President and
Chief Executive Officer*

Gilbert M. Grosvenor
Chairman of the Board

Nina D. Hoffman
*Executive Vice President
President, Books and
Education Publishing Group*

Ericka Markman
*Senior Vice President
President, Children's Books and
Education Publishing Group*

Stephen Mico
*Senior Vice President
Publisher, Children's Books and
Education Publishing Group*

Staff for this book

Nancy Laties Feresten
*Vice President
Editor-in-Chief, Children's Books
Project Editor*

Bea Jackson
*Design Director, Children's Books and
Education Publishing Group*

David M. Seager
Designer, Children's Books

Margaret Sidlosky
*Photography Director, Children's Books and
Education Publishing Group*

Jean Cantu
Illustrations coordinator

Lewis R. Bassford
Production Manager

Priyanka Lamichhane
Editorial Assistant

Vincent P. Ryan
Manufacturing Manager

Connie Binder
Indexer

Design by Christopher Sloan

Principal consultants

Luis Chiappe, Ph.D.
*Chairman, Department of Vertebrate
Paleontology, Curator, Natural History
Museum of Los Angeles County*

Kevin Padian, Ph.D.
*Professor of Integrative Biology, University
of California, Berkeley*

Richard Prum, Ph.D.
*William Robertson Coe Professor of
Ornithology, Ecology, and Evolutionary
Biology, Peabody Museum of Natural
History, Yale University*

Hans-Dieter Sues, Ph.D.
*Associate Director for Research and
Collections, Smithsonian Institution
National Museum of Natural History.
Committee for Research and Exploration,
National Geographic Society*

Xu Xing, Ph.D.
*Institute of Vertebrate Paleontology and
Paleoanthropology, Beijing, China*

Acknowledgments

Without the contributions of
many knowledgeable and talented
individuals, this book would not
have been possible. I thank them
all for their support. I feel especially
privileged to have shared this project with Dr. Xu Xing. Few have as
much firsthand experience with
the discovery and study of
Chinese feathered dinosaurs as he
and his colleagues of the Institute
of Vertebrate Paleontology and
Paleoanthropology in Beijing.
Likewise, Dr. Mark Norell at the
American Museum of Natural
History has always been generous
with his time and valuable advice
on this complex subject.

I would also like to thank
sculptor Alan Groves for his
enthusiastic involvement in this
project and for his wonderful
artwork that appears in this book.

**Library of Congress
Cataloging-in-Publication Data**
is available from the Library of Congress
upon request.

Trade ISBN: 0-7922-7298-6

Library Binding ISBN: 0-7922-7404-0

Printed in the U.S.A.

Contents

A feathered dinosaur, *Sinornithosaurus,* leaps through the air to grab some dinner in this model.

In this scene from prehistoric China, the primitive bird *Jeholornis* (right) faces off with the dinosaur *Microraptor zhaoianus* while the dinosaur *Sinornithosaurus* chases the primitive bird *Confuciusornis*.

Introduction

For many people, dinosaurs mean gigantic animals. But they are wrong. Although many dinosaurs are super sized, there are a lot of small dinosaurs as well, and these often play a key role in the evolutionary history of dinosaurs. This is clearly seen with the example of bird origins. In this case, a group of predatory dinosaurs became smaller and smaller in size, gradually acquired bird features, and finally evolved into the first bird. From that ancestor rose the diverse bird family that includes all living birds today.

This understanding is based on literally tons of fossil evidence from all over the world. In these fossils we can see many similarities between the skeletons of birds and dinosaurs and in the microstructure of bone and eggshell. We can even see similarities in the behavior of dinosaurs and birds. Yet the discovery of feathers on dinosaurs is still the most obvious way to link the two groups.

In 1996, *Sinosauropteryx*, the first dinosaur in the world found with fluffy primitive feathers, was reported from Liaoning Province, China. Since then new feathered dinosaur species have been found in the same area and the number of reported species is now up to ten. My colleagues and I have been lucky enough to discover and name six of them, including the bizarre therizinosaur *Beipiaosaurus*, the fearsome tyrannosaur *Dilong*, and the weird dromaeosaur *Microraptor gui*, a tiny dinosaur bearing long flight feathers on its legs.

These discoveries clearly show that the dinosaurian ancestor of birds had already evolved key bird features, including small size, feathers, and wings, before the first bird ever flew into the blue sky. These discoveries also provide the strongest evidence that birds are indeed descendants of ancient dinosaurs. With the new discoveries from Liaoning, there is no doubt that a dinosaurian lineage survived the big extinction at the end of Cretaceous period and that we are living in a dinosaurian world.

Dr. Xu Xing

Institute for Vertebrate Paleontology and Paleoanthropology, Beijing, China

Much new information about the origins of flight has come from China, where Dr. Xu Xing (above, with *Microraptor gui*) studies the transition from dinosaurs to birds.

Hummingbirds are big eaters, having to eat as much as 1.5 to 3 times their weight in nectar and insects per day. This bird's distant relative, *Tyrannosaurus rex*, was a well-known big eater, too.

THE CASE FOR BIRDS AS DINOSAURS

It is hard to imagine that a hummingbird, one of the smallest and most delicate of birds, is a relative of *Tyrannosaurus rex*, one of the biggest and fiercest dinosaurs that ever lived, but it's true. How do we know? After all, we see birds all the time but all we have of dinosaurs is their fossils—bones, eggs, footprints, droppings, and other remains that were buried and then turned to stone.

Learning about prehistoric life through fossils and other evidence is a lot like solving a mystery. Paleontologists—the scientists who study dinosaurs and other fossils—have two basic jobs. They collect evidence. (That's the part that involves camping in deserts and digging bones from the ground with dental picks.) And they analyze evidence. (That's what happens when they get all that stuff back to the laboratory, unwrap it, piece it together, and compare it with things that other paleontologists have found as well as with living animals.) Based on that analysis, they come up with a hypothesis—an idea that explains all the evidence. This is exactly what's been happening as paleontologists work to solve the case of birds and dinosaurs.

evidence: Something that can be shown to support a proposed idea. In paleontology, the evidence is often from fossils, but important forms of evidence also come from other sources, such as the science of genetics and the study of living animals.

hypothesis, hypotheses: A hypothesis is a temporary conclusion used to explain certain facts. As more evidence is unearthed, a hypothesis might be either supported or rejected. The plural of hypothesis is hypotheses. In cases where there is more than one hypothesis, the one that makes the fewest complicated assumptions is considered most likely to be true. That's how science works.

Words to Know

7

Are birds descended from dinosaurs?

The idea that birds descended from dinosaurs has not always been as widely accepted among scientists as it is today. In the 1860s, British scientist Thomas Henry Huxley pointed to the similarities of the bones of birds and dinosaurs when the remains of *Archaeopteryx*—a bird that lived 150 million years ago—had just been discovered. This evidence, he said, supported the hypothesis that birds were the descendants of dinosaurs. Some scientists agreed with him, but others strongly opposed him. Why? Because many people did not accept the possibility that one species could change into another over time.

At the root of the disagreement was British scientist Charles Darwin's theory that evolution—change over time—occurs by a mechanism called natural selection. He described how one species could descend, or evolve, from another over time in his book *On the Origin of Species*. Edward Cope, a well-known American paleontologist, and Huxley agreed that Darwin's theory of how evolution occurs explained how some dinosaurs could have gradually changed toward more birdlike forms and eventually into real birds, such as *Archaeopteryx*.

Richard Owen, shown above with the skeleton of an extinct bird known as a moa, did not agree with Darwin's view of how species evolve.

EVIDENCE: *Archaeopteryx* gave scientists the first evidence of what the earliest birds were like. Over millions of years the bones of *Archaeopteryx* had been transformed into a fossil. Yet the fossil of *Archaeopteryx* was very unusual. The stone that surrounded the body of *Archaeopteryx* was so fine-grained that it preserved not only the bones, but impressions of its feathers as well. This was the first time feathers had been seen on a prehistoric creature. Otherwise, however, *Archaeopteryx* was very similar to small theropod dinosaurs, such as *Compsognathus*.

HYPOTHESIS 1: *Archaeopteryx*, with its sharp teeth, clawed fingers, and long bony tail, could easily be classified as a small dinosaur. Huxley therefore hypothesized that birds descended from dinosaurs.

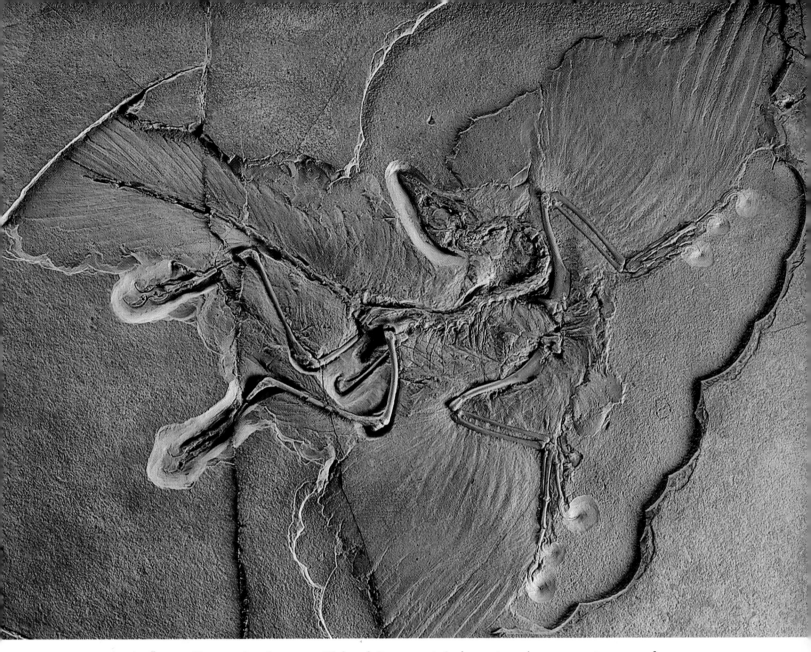

Despite its many dinosaurian features, Richard Owen put *Archaeopteryx* in a separate group from dinosaurs when it was classified in the 1860s.

HYPOTHESIS 2: Another British scientist of the time, Richard Owen, disagreed strongly with Darwin and Huxley's view of how one species could evolve from another over long periods of time. Instead of pointing to the similarities between dinosaurs and birds, he pointed at the differences. One proof that birds were clearly different from all other animals, he said, was that birds had feathers and no other living thing did. Birds were members of the scientific classification Aves (Aves is the Latin word for birds), and dinosaurs were members of the scientific classification Reptilia, where he himself had decided they belonged 20 years before. Owen placed *Archaeopteryx* firmly into Aves and would go no further. His hypothesis was that *Archaeopteryx* was a bird, plain and simple.

Is *Deinonychus* a clue to the ancestry of birds?

From Owen's time until recently, most scientists accepted that birds and dinosaurs were separate in the Animal Kingdom. Things started to shift back toward the views of Huxley in the early 1970s, when an American scientist named John Ostrom brought new attention to the similarities between dinosaurs and birds.

EVIDENCE: Ostrom was studying a carnivorous dinosaur, *Deinonychus*, that had just been named. He noticed that the bones of *Deinonychus* were very similar to those of *Archaeopteryx* and also to those of living birds.

Since then, other studies have provided new kinds of evidence and new methods of analysis. Among these are studies of microscopic bone structure and growth rates, the chemical composition of feathers, and growth patterns of bird embryos. In one rare case, soft tissue of a *Tyrannosaurus rex*—*T. rex* for short— was preserved within a fossilized bone. The tissue was found to be very similar to tissue found in ostriches. Amid this wealth of strong new evidence that birds descended from dinosaurs, the very strongest is a collection of dinosaur fossils from China preserved with the impressions of feathers surrounding their bodies.

HYPOTHESIS: Birds and dinosaurs are closely related and should be in the same class. The feathery fossils from China and other evidence have convinced most scientists that Huxley and Cope were right long ago—birds are descended from dinosaurs.

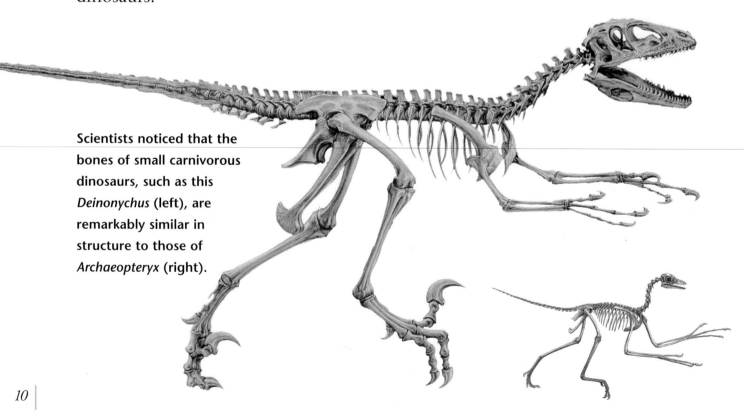

Scientists noticed that the bones of small carnivorous dinosaurs, such as this *Deinonychus* (left), are remarkably similar in structure to those of *Archaeopteryx* (right).

The fossil remains of several *Deinonychus* have been found near the bones of a *Tenontosaurus*, an ornithischian dinosaur. It is possible that the *Deinonychus* had attacked the sauropod as a group, as shown in this model.

THE FEATHERED DINOSAURS

What's all the fuss about? Since 1996 a parade of dinosaur fossils found in China has been attracting a lot of attention. Most of the fossils are about 125 million years old and come from a region in northeastern China called Liaoning Province. The way the fossils were preserved happened to preserve feathers as well as bones, and on many specimens a variety of feather types can be seen. Some of the feathers are small and fuzzy. Others are long and have a remarkable

Tyrannosaurus rex
This dinosaur has **not** been found with feathers... yet.

Beipiaosaurus
A feathered
therizinosaur

◀ **THEROPODS FURTHER FROM BIRDS**

12

Sinosauropteryx
A feathered
theropod

Dilong
A feathered
tyrannosaur

Shuvuuia
A feathered
maniraptor

Caudipteryx
A feathered close
relative of oviraptors

resemblance to those found on birds today. In fact, many of the fossils found at Liaoning are bird fossils. The feathers, both long and short, that were preserved on many of the bird fossils look similar to feathers found on the fossils of dinosaurs that were not birds.

So far, all of the feathered dinosaurs found belong to one group, the theropods. We'll learn more about them in the next chapter.

New feathered fossils are being discovered frequently, but when this book was written, this is what the list looked like. The feathered theropod most distantly related to birds is at far left. Living birds, represented by a crow, are shown on the right. While *Dilong*, a tyrannosaur, has been found with feathers, its close relative *T. rex* has not. *T. rex* is shown here only for scale.

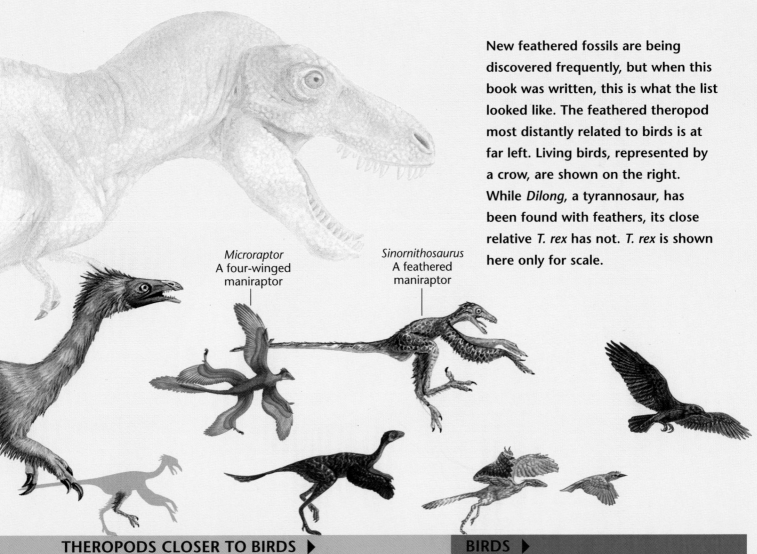

Microraptor
A four-winged maniraptor

Sinornithosaurus
A feathered maniraptor

THEROPODS CLOSER TO BIRDS ▶

Pedopenna
A maniraptor with feathery feet

Protarchaeopteryx
A feathered maniraptor

BIRDS ▶

Archaeopteryx
The first bird

Eoalulavis
An early bird

Corvus (crow)
A living bird

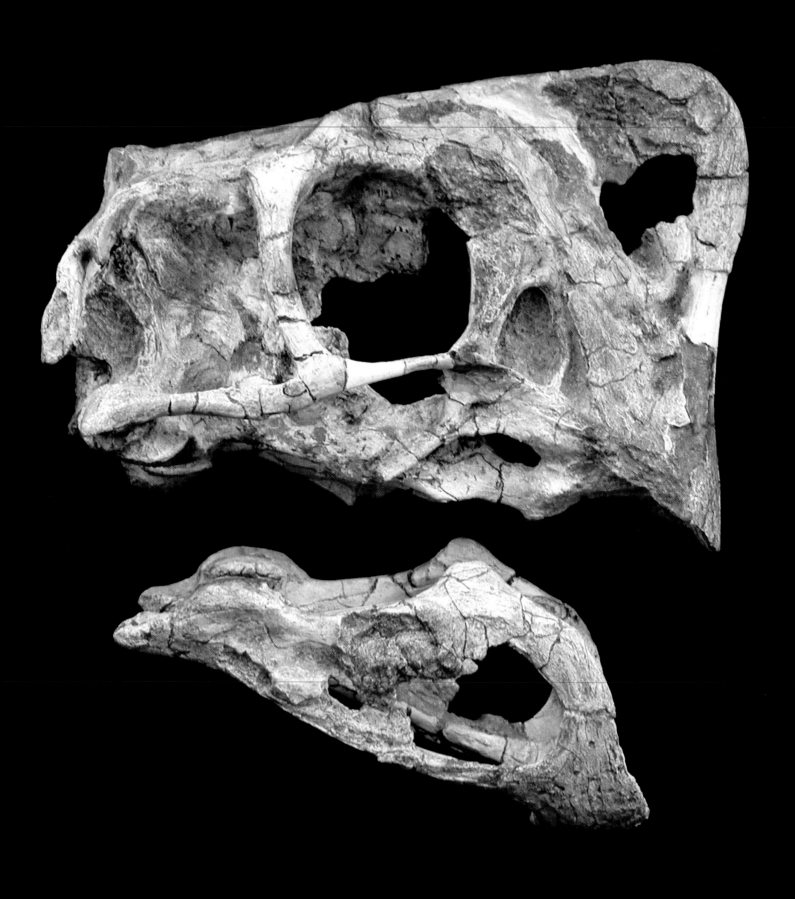

This beaked maniraptor theropod, known as *Oviraptor*, bears a strong superficial resemblance to living birds, such as the parrot or cassowary. Yet other theropods were more closely related to birds.

WHAT KIND OF DINOSAURS ARE BIRDS?

Scientists have now generally accepted the idea that birds are dinosaurs and are trying to answer other puzzling questions that this concept raises. The big question explored in this chapter is "What kind of dinosaurs are birds?"

All of the feathered dinosaurs are from one subgroup known as the theropods. Among the theropods are the dinosaurs that are the most birdlike of all, without actually being birds. They are the maniraptors. Most maniraptors were predators with flexible arms and hands that gave them their name, which means "hand thief." They were able to fold their long arms along their sides just like birds.

Maniraptors came in a wide range of sizes. Some were the size of crows, but others were much bigger. *Utahraptor* from North America was more than 20 feet long. Compared to other dinosaurs, such as the long-necked sauropods, maniraptors had large brains. Larger brains would later be very important as dinosaurs took flight, because it would take extra brain power to navigate through the air.

Two groups of maniraptors were even more birdlike than others. These were the dromaeosaurs and the troodontids. Of the two groups, dromaeosaurs appear to be the most similar to what the common ancestor of birds was like. There were many groups of early birds that descended from this common ancestor, but only one—the Neornithes, or neornithines—is living today.

avian, nonavian If birds are dinosaurs, the phrase "birds and dinosaurs" doesn't make sense. To be clear about the difference between birds and *other* dinosaurs, scientists use the word "avian" to refer to birds. The rest of the dinosaurs are "nonavian."

Mesozoic Era The time between 248 million years ago and 65 million years ago is called the Mesozoic Era. It is divided into three periods: the Triassic, Jurassic, and Cretaceous. We live in the Cenozoic Era, which immediately followed the Mesozoic.

Words to Know

Where do dinosaurs come from?

Scientists place dinosaurs, birds, crocodiles, and pterosaurs (an extinct flying reptile) in a group called archosaurs. They evolved in the first part of the Mesozoic Era, the Triassic period, which lasted from 248 million to 206 million years ago. Archosaurs, meaning "ruling reptiles," dominated the land in the Triassic period, and they still dominate the land today in the form of birds.

EVIDENCE: One trait that all archosaurs share is an opening in their skulls in front of each eye. Turtles, snakes, lizards, mammals, and other animals do not have this hole. Dinosaurs do.

HYPOTHESIS: Dinosaurs, including birds, evolved from early archosaurs.

Note the archosaur opening in front of the eye in *T. rex.*

There is wide agreement among scientists that birds evolved from earlier archosaurs, just as crocodiles and pterosaurs did. And there is overwhelming evidence that the path to birds leads through the dinosaur lineage of archosaurs.

Avian theropod dinosaurs (birds) —

Nonavian theropod dinosaurs

Maniraptors

Theropods

Tyrannosaurs

Saurischians

Brachiosaurus

Dinosaurs

Sauropods (long-necked dinosaurs)

Early archosaurs

Ornithischians (duckbill dinosaurs, horned dinosaurs)

Pterosaurs

Crocodiles

PALEOZOIC ERA		MESOZOIC ERA	
Time (millions of years ago)	Triassic Period	Jurassic Period	
	248 213		

Which dinosaurs are the most likely ancestors of birds?

Long before scientists were certain that birds descended from dinosaurs, they were naming dinosaurs for their birdlike qualities. Ironically, of the two main divisions of dinosaurs, the one known as the ornithischian, or bird-hipped, dinosaurs had little to do with bird evolution. The other group did. These were the saurischian, or lizard-hipped, dinosaurs. This second group is divided between the long-necked sauropods and the meat-eating theropods.

Many nonavian theropods were so birdlike that they were named for birds. One group, for example, is the ornithomimosaurs, or bird-mimic reptiles. Among these are *Gallimimus*, *Struthiomimus*, and *Pelicanimimus*. These are named for their resemblance to chickens, ostriches, and pelicans, respectively.

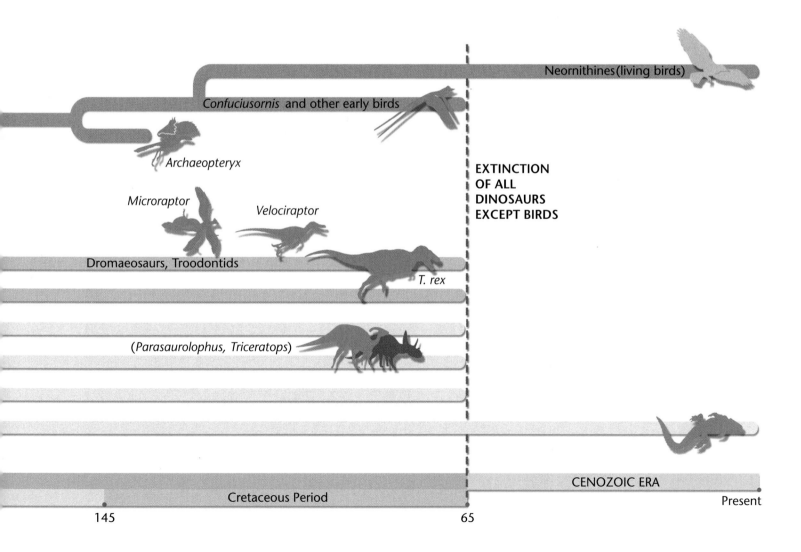

Neornithines (living birds)

Confuciusornis and other early birds

Archaeopteryx

Microraptor

Velociraptor

EXTINCTION OF ALL DINOSAURS EXCEPT BIRDS

Dromaeosaurs, Troodontids

T. rex

(*Parasaurolophus*, *Triceratops*)

CENOZOIC ERA

Cretaceous Period

Present

145

65

We can see that this fossil troodon, Mei long (above), tucked its head behind its arm while resting. Today's warm-blooded birds, such as the swan shown below, do this to keep warm. One interpretation of this evidence is that troodontids might have been warm-blooded like birds.

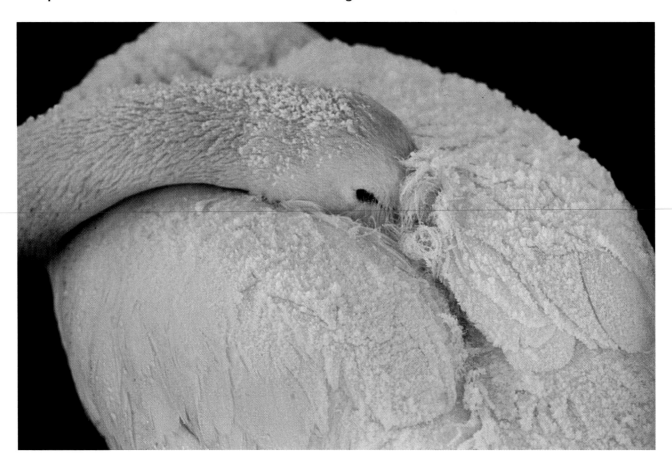

EVIDENCE: One can see the beginnings of bird-like body plans among the earliest dinosaurs that lived 230 million years ago in the Triassic period. *Coelophysis*, for example, had feet like a bird, was a fast runner, and had a lightweight skull posted on a flexible "S"-curved neck.

Coelophysis and all early dinosaurs also walked on two legs tucked directly under the body just like birds. There are not many animals that walk on two legs like this. Dinosaurs and humans are among the few. Over millions of years, several groups of dinosaurs returned to walking on all fours, but not the theropods. They stayed on two legs.

The word theropod means "beast foot," a name that comes from these dinosaurs' feet, which have three large clawed toes. All theropods walked on these three toes, but they also had a small first toe called a hallux. Bird feet are the same, but in perching birds the hallux is twisted to be opposite the front three toes like a thumb. This is important for grasping branches. Theropods had three clawed fingers also. These were good for grasping prey.

Bird and theropod bones are similar in other ways. Two studies of the microscopic structure of dinosaur and bird bones showed that *T. rex*, and all other theropods, grew very fast, just as large

Therizinosaurs were bizarre theropods with three large clawed fingers, tiny teeth, and feathers. This drawing shows them using their claws for fighting, but no one knows for sure exactly what they were for.

UNSOLVED MYSTERY!

living birds do. *T. rex* could pack on as much as four and a half pounds a day.

Large theropods, such as *T. rex*, are only distantly related to birds. Most evidence suggests that small, fast dromaeosaurs and troodontids, members of a subgroup of theropods known as maniraptors, are closer relatives. *Velociraptor* and *Deinonychus* are perhaps the best-known of the dromaeosaurs. Among the troodontids are *Troodon*, which gave the group its name, and *Sinornithoides*, meaning "Chinese bird form." *Mei long*, a dinosaur found fossilized in a sleeping position, was also a troodontid.

HYPOTHESIS: Birds descended from theropod dinosaurs, most likely from an ancestor shared with dromaeosaurs or troodontids.

Dromaeosaur
(*Velociraptor*)

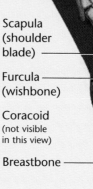

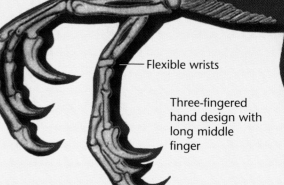

Scapula
(shoulder
blade)

Furcula
(wishbone)

Coracoid
(not visible
in this view)

Breastbone

Flexible wrists

Three-fingered
hand design with
long middle
finger

BONE CLONES?

Scientists have a long list of features that maniraptors, such as this *Velociraptor*, have in common with birds. Check this list of evidence and the anatomy that birds and dinosaurs share (right) to see if you agree with the scientists that birds are mani-raptor dinosaurs.

thin-walled, hollow bones: Unlike the bones of crocodiles, turtles, and mammals, maniraptor bones were relatively thin-walled and hollow. Bird bones are even more so.

tails: Although *Velociraptor* has a long tail, some maniraptors, such as *Beipiaosaurus*, a feathered therizinosaur, have primitive pygostyles, the bony stump that living birds have.

toe claws: Dromaeosaurs and troodontids had a large sickle-shape toe claw on each foot. One early bird fossil, *Rahonavis*, has toes like this as well.

shoulder girdle: The shoulder girdle in some of the maniraptors is basically the same as those seen in early birds. It is made up of the scapula, the coracoid, and the furcula or wishbone.

wrist: There is a half-moon-shaped bone in both maniraptor and bird wrists that allows these animals to fold their arms tightly back to their bodies after rapidly extending them forward. Nonavian maniraptors may have used this motion to grab prey. It is key to the flight stroke of birds.

Crow

Scientists count more than 100 similarities between nonavian maniraptor dinosaurs, such as *Velociraptor,* and birds. This art shows just a few of them.

Flexible wrists

Three-fingered hand design with long middle finger

Scapula (shoulder blade)

Furcula (wishbone)

Coracoid

Breastbone

Backward-pointing pubis

Pygostyle

Backward-pointing pubis

Hallux

Three forward-pointing toes and a hallux

Hallux

Three forward-pointing toes and a hallux

Were the downlike structures on Chinese fossils, such as this one, nicknamed "Dave," true feathers? The scientists who studied this fossil announced that there was no doubt that the answer was yes.

DINO-FUZZ AND OTHER FEATHER MYSTERIES

Feathers had never been seen on anything but a bird until the first feathered dinosaur from China, *Sinosauropteryx*, was announced in 1996. Of all the evidence that supported the hypothesis of a close link between dinosaurs and birds, none was as convincing as this. Still, some scientists were skeptical. They suggested that what appeared to be downlike feathers was something else— perhaps fibers of collagen, the protein that makes up cartilage and tendons. They called the suspicious material "dino-fuzz."

Since then, much work has been done to establish the true nature of the downlike structures on *Sinosauropteryx* and other feathered dinosaurs. Many other feathered dinosaurs, such as *Protarchaeopteryx*, *Caudipteryx*, and *Shuvuuia*, have since been found and have added important new evidence. Much work has also been done to understand the structure of feathers and how they grow. Just what dino-fuzz is and what it has to do with the appearance of feathers in birds are the big questions of this chapter.

basal vs. primitive vs. early

basal: An animal that is basal is one that is closer to the "base" of the evolutionary tree than another animal it is being compared to. The opposite of basal is advanced.

primitive: Features of an animal, such as the number of fingers on a hand, can be called primitive, but the animal itself cannot. The opposite of primitive is derived, which means the trait has undergone evolutionary change.

early: This word is used to describe time. The opposite of early is late.

Words to Know

When did feathers first evolve?

EVIDENCE: The earliest known feathers are from the Jurassic period, which lasted from 206 million to 144 million years ago. Until recently, the only fossil feathers from this time were from the earliest known bird, *Archaeopteryx*. It lived about 150 million years ago. Recently the fossilized foot of a newly discovered nonavian dinosaur, *Pedopenna daohugouensis*, joined *Archaeopteryx* as the only other feathered fossil from that period. There is still some question about how old the rocky layers where it came from in Inner Mongolia are, but if the reported age of 164 million years holds up, the feathers of *Pedopenna* will become the oldest known, beating *Archaeopteryx* by some 14 million years.

PROBLEM: These Jurassic feathers give us the time feathers first appear in the fossil record, but not the time when they first evolved. And even though the feathers of *Archaeopteryx* and *Pedopenna* are the earliest known, they are not primitive in form. They look just like those of living birds.

The advanced feathers of *Archaeopteryx* and *Pedopenna* present a problem because they appear millions of years *before* dinosaurs with dino-fuzz. Many scientists suggest dino-fuzz is a primitive form of feather. But if dino-fuzz is a form of primitive feather, why does it only appear millions of years *after* the advanced feathers of *Archaeopteryx* and *Pedopenna*? At first glance the cart seems to be before the horse.

This is not as big a problem as you might think, however. Animals with primitive traits often survive into eras alongside or beyond more advanced animals. Monotremes such as the platypus, for example, are a form of living mammal that still has the primitive trait of laying eggs. They have stuck with it for the last 110 million years. So some dinosaurs living 125

Pedopenna is the only feathery fossil known from the Jurassic period other than *Archaeopteryx*. Experts can identify this fragment as a very early maniraptor dinosaur. The feathers radiate to the left from the long bone.

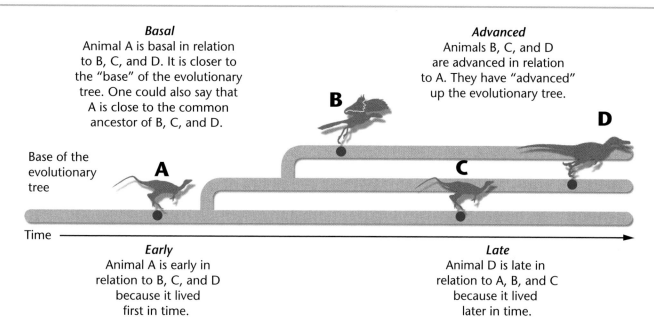

Basal
Animal A is basal in relation to B, C, and D. It is closer to the "base" of the evolutionary tree. One could also say that A is close to the common ancestor of B, C, and D.

Advanced
Animals B, C, and D are advanced in relation to A. They have "advanced" up the evolutionary tree.

Base of the evolutionary tree

A

B

C

D

Time

Early
Animal A is early in relation to B, C, and D because it lived first in time.

Late
Animal D is late in relation to A, B, and C because it lived later in time.

This diagram shows how it is possible for nonavian feathered dinosaurs, such as *Sinosauropteryx* (C) and *Velociraptor* (D), to live beyond the time when flight feathers might have evolved in other theropods, such as *Archaeopteryx* (B). All of these animals must have descended from a feathery common ancestor (A). *Sinosauropteryx* simply did not change much from the form of the common ancestor. In that sense, when *Sinosauropteryx* was alive, it was already a "living fossil."

million years ago may have been like the platypus, keeping primitive traits—in this case, dino-fuzz—millions of years after more derived feathers had appeared on the scene in other animals, such as *Archaeopteryx* and *Pedopenna*.

HYPOTHESIS: Because *Archaeopteryx*'s and *Pedopenna*'s feathers are so advanced, they must have had millions of years to evolve from a more primitive form. The dino-fuzz on feathered dinosaurs may be what primitive feathers looked like, even though its first appearance in the fossil record is millions of years later than the advanced feathers of *Archaeopteryx* and *Pedopenna*. Feathers earlier than these, however, have yet to be discovered.

UNSOLVED MYSTERY!

The echidna, or spiny anteater, is a good example of an animal living today that has held onto a very primitive trait. Like the earliest mammals that lived millions of years ago, it lays eggs.

Sinosauropteryx, shown here in a reconstruction, was the first feathered nonavian dinosaur discovered. Its downy coat of dino-fuzz, or primitive feathers, may have provided camouflage and warmth.

What did the most primitive feathers look like?

EVIDENCE: *Sinosauropteryx* was the first feathered dinosaur discovered. It was a small-bodied animal covered with dino-fuzz, which under a magnifying glass appears fluffy, like the down feathers of birds. Many of the nonavian feathered dinosaur fossils from China have the same fuzz, even when they also have other, more complex feathers. A lot of the fossilized birds from China, such as the thousands of specimens of *Confuciusornis*, also have fuzz preserved.

Because *Sinosauropteryx* is a basal dinosaur when compared to some of the other feathered theropods from China, establishing just what its fuzzy coat was made of was important. If it could be shown that *Sinosauropteryx*'s fuzz was definitely feathers, then scientists would have strong evidence of what primitive feathers looked like.

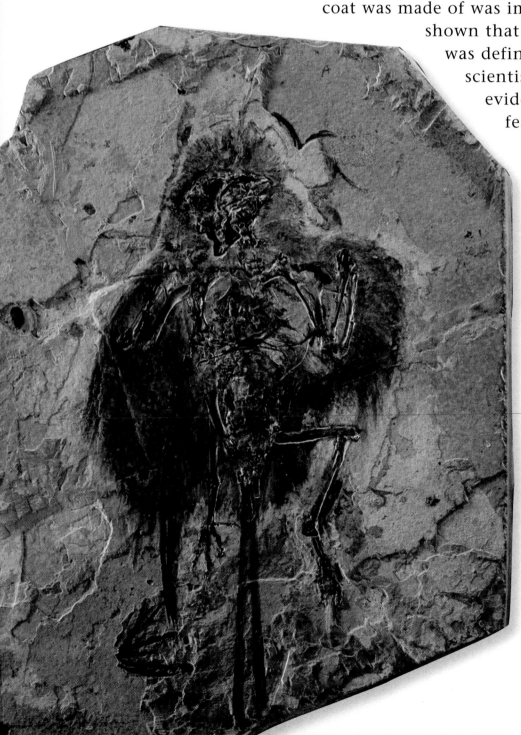

Chemical analysis was attempted but was not successful. Microscopic inspection of these structures revealed that they were very simple and hairlike in structure. Some scientists reported seeing branching, evidence that *Sinosauropteryx*'s downy coat was feathers and not something else. Not everyone was convinced, however.

Bird fossils from Liaoning Province, such as this *Changchengornis,* often show the same fuzzy covering that *Sinosauropteryx* had.

No one knows what the fuzzy coat of *Sinosauropteryx* was like in life, but scientists suggest that it might have looked something like the coat of a kiwi (above), a ground-dwelling bird from New Zealand that has hairlike feathers. A magnified view of the fuzz on *Sinosauropteryx* (below) shows that at first glance it is like the softer feathers, such as down, on living birds.

Look at the picture at the right and decide for yourself.

HYPOTHESIS: Small-bodied dinosaurs were the first creatures to have feathers. Their "protofeathers" had a simple hairlike structure. The fact that the advanced feathers of *Archaeopteryx* and *Pedopenna* existed before the primitive feathers of *Sinosauropteryx* suggests that while advanced feathers evolved in some creatures, others kept the simple feathers of the common ancestor.

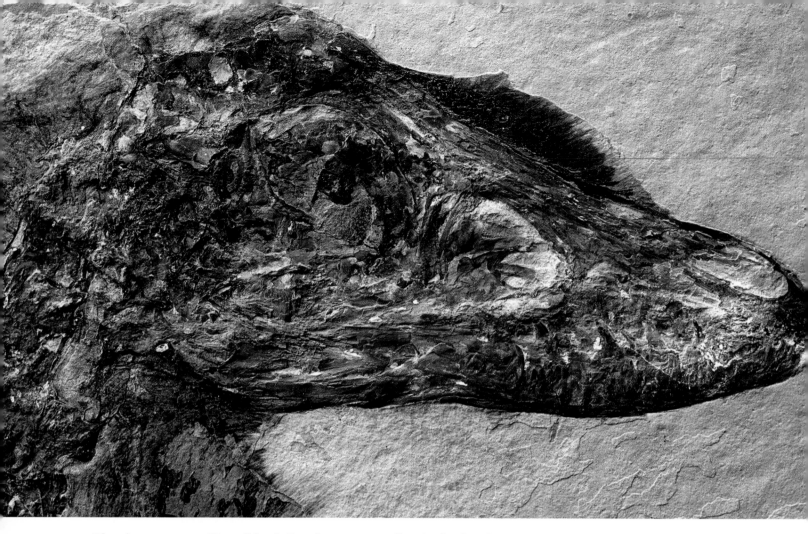

The dromaeosaur "Dave" had dino-fuzz surrounding its body. The preservation of this fossil was so good that scientists were able to show that dino-fuzz had a structure unique to feathers.

Was "dino-fuzz" a form of primitive feather?

Until 1999 chemical analysis of the hairlike structures on fossils from China had been impossible because every part of the fossil had been completely turned to mineral. Chemical analysis requires that some trace of the animal's flesh, bones, or in this case, feathers, be preserved, and this is rare in dinosaur fossils. Proving that there was branching in the fine downy structures had been tough as well. But two discoveries in 1999 and 2000 led to new breakthroughs.

Shuvuuia was a strange nonavian maniraptor with a greatly enlarged thumb.

EVIDENCE: A dinosaur fossil found in Mongolia in 1993 looked like it might still have featherlike structures that had not been turned completely to stone. The fossil of the new dinosaur, *Shuvuuia*, had been found surrounded by small hollow fibers scientists thought might be the remains of bristle feathers. No one was sure whether tissues of this animal that died 80 million years ago could still be tested for the chemical signature of feathers, but they were going to try. They would be looking for signs of a protein group called beta-keratins.

Beta-keratin proteins are found not only in feathers but also in claws, beaks, and scales around the eyes and on the feet of birds. These proteins are very different from alpha-keratins, which are found in skin, hair, and fur. If beta-keratins could be found in the bristle-like structures on *Shuvuuia*, it would be strong evidence that they were true feathers.

In 1999 the results of the *Shuvuuia* chemical testing were announced. It showed that the structures were most likely made of beta-keratin proteins.

In 2000 a young dromaeosaur was found in China with dino-fuzz covering its 24-inch body from head to tail. It was nicknamed "Dave." In some places on Dave's body, there were tufts of these structures. Along the back of the arms scientists could see clearly that these structures each had a rachis and barbs, just like modern bird feathers (see page 34).

HYPOTHESIS: The hairlike structures or dino-fuzz seen on the nonavian dinosaurs from China and in *Shuvuuia* from Mongolia are true feathers.

The longest hairlike structures on Dave's body were found on its arms, as shown in this illustration.

How did feathers evolve into their present form?

The origin of feathers

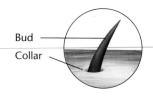

Bud
Collar

Step 1: The first stage in the evolution of feathers was a cone-shaped bud in a circular collar of skin.

Barb closeup

Step 2: Hairlike structures called barbs form in a circle around the collar. These open up to form a downy feather similar to what can be found on baby birds.

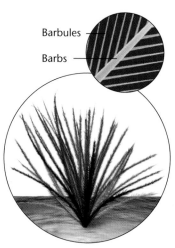

Barbules
Barbs

Step 3: Smaller structures called barbules form along the barbs. Barbs with their barbules can also form along a central shaft, called a rachis. This can give a feather the appearance of being suitable for flying, but it is not yet ready.

Barbules
Barbs
Rachis

Barbules
Hooklets
Barb

Step 4: Hooklets on the barbules help close the barbs together, making an "air proof" feather—a critical thing for flight.

It is very difficult to say what specific biological processes came into play long ago to produce the first feathers and the hairlike structures on dinosaurs such as Dave. Scientists can, however, study the bodies of living animals to figure out how such things could have occurred through changes in genetic chemistry. These are the sort of changes that over generations could—and did—change the appearance of animals and even produce new species. Recent research has shown that genes are powerful agents of change and that major changes, such as additional pairs of legs in arthropods, can be triggered by simple genetic switches.

EVIDENCE: A study of chickens showed that small changes to their genetic chemistry could cause feathers to grow from the surface of scales on their feet. Another study showed how the rachis and barbs are con-trolled by simple chemical signals. By changing the signals, scientists could control the size and shape of the rachis and make the barbs appear or disappear. Several similar studies reinforced these results.

HYPOTHESIS: Feathers first evolved through simple changes in genetic chemistry over millions of years. These changes to the primitive growth process probably occurred in a stepwise fashion.

Why did feathers evolve?

No one knows why the first feathers evolved, but they certainly helped small animals stay warm once they became a full body covering. To understand what other advantages early feathers might have provided, scientists look to living birds.

EVIDENCE: In living birds, downlike feathers are used in the following ways:
• Nestling birds today are often covered in downy feathers. These keep their small bodies warm.
• Modern nestlings' feathers are often colored to hide them from predators.
• Modern birds—flightless and flying—use many types of feathers for recognizing animals of the same species and attracting mates.

HYPOTHESIS: The first feathers were not useful for flight but were perhaps useful for keeping small-bodied dinosaurs warm. Other purposes, such as camouflage, recognizing other animals of the same species, and attracting mates, must be considered as well.

Whether or not a genetic trait, such as the fancy collar on this pigeon, is an advantage to an animal or not can sometimes determine if the trait is passed on to later generations.

WHAT ARE FEATHERS?

Feathers are one of the most complex skin structures known. This is one reason why scientists like Richard Owen put birds in a class of their own. Feathers come in five basic forms. All of these can be seen on birds living today, and all but one—filoplumes—have been found preserved in nonavian dinosaur fossils.

All feathers, whatever their type and however they are used, are made up of these same structures:

Vane

Rachis

Calamus

A pheasant's tail flight feather.

shaft: The central support of a feather.
calamus: The base of the shaft.
rachis: The upper portion of the shaft.
vane: The feathery part on either side of the shaft. It is formed by many parallel rows of barbs.
barbs: The hairlike structures that stick out sideways from the rachis.
barbules: Small structures that stick out sideways from each barb toward the barb that is next to it.
hooklets: Structures at the ends of some barbules that are shaped so they clasp onto the barbule of the next barb. This hooking mechanism, sort of like velcro, is what makes a feather hold its shape so well. If the hooklets become undone, the bird can "rezip" them by sliding its feathers through its beak. Some feathers do not "zip," which makes them fluffy. Some nestlings have down that doesn't even have a rachis. These very simple feathers are extra fluffy.

A contour feather with a downy base from a partridge.

Basic types of feathers

Contour feathers are flat feathers that cover the body of the bird, giving it a streamlined form.

Flight feathers are the long feathers of the wings and tail. They have the same general form as contour feathers, but the vanes on either side of the rachis are unequal in width. This helps create the forces that birds need to fly.

Down feathers are soft tufts that are usually found closest to a bird's skin. They are so soft and warm they are often used in blankets, sleeping bags, and coats.

Filoplumes are hairlike in shape but have a very small vane at the end. These feathers are sensitive to pressure and vibration. The hairlike structures you see on a plucked chicken are filoplumes.

Bristles are hairlike but are different from filoplumes in that they are stiff and do not have a vane at the end. They can be found on a bird's face.

This assortment of feathers allows a bird to fly, protects its delicate skin, and keeps it warm and dry. In many cases, feathers have evolved into specialized forms. Waterbird feathers are waterproof. Owls have feathers shaped to make their flight soundless and other feathers by their ears to improve their hearing. Some birds use their feathers to make courtship sounds that attract mates. Desert sandgrouse even use their breast feathers to soak up water and carry it to their nestlings miles away.

Barbs

Rachis

A peacock feather showing the barbs and, in a magnified view, the barbules.

This fossil of *Sinosauropteryx* stunned scientists when photographs of it were shown at a meeting in 1999. Although hundreds of dinosaurs had been discovered, none had yet been found with feathers.

BIRDS' CLOSEST KIN

Although many scientists were convinced that birds were dinosaurs long before the first feathered dinosaur was found, they only dreamed that a feathery fossil like *Sinosauropteryx* would ever be discovered. So there was much amazement when, after the already astonishing discovery of *Sinosauropteryx*, a nonstop stream of feathery dinosaurs started pouring out from Liaoning Province in eastern China. Ancient mud and volcanic ash there, turned to stone over millions of years, preserved leaves and other delicate plant parts, the wings of insects, and the feathers of dinosaurs.

The known feathered dinosaurs come from many different groups of theropods. Some of them, such as dromaeosaurs, were known to be closely related to birds, so in a way, feathers were not a big surprise when they were found on *Sinornithosaurus*, a very birdlike dromaeosaur. But feathers were also found on relatives of *Oviraptor*, tyrannosaurs, therizinosaurs, and other dinosaurs that scientists view as less closely related to birds. This raises the questions of how many different types of theropods had feathers and when they might have first appeared among this group. In this chapter we'll look at these questions and ask which of the feathered dinosaurs from China is most closely related to birds.

symmetrical There are two forms of long contour feathers that are important for this chapter. Symmetrical feathers have vanes of similar width on each side of the rachis. Scientists suggest this form of feather came before asymmetrical feathers.

asymmetrical Asymmetrical feathers have uneven vane widths on either side of the rachis. The flight feathers of birds are asymmetrical. Asymmetrical feathers are very important for creating the forces needed for flight.

Words to Know

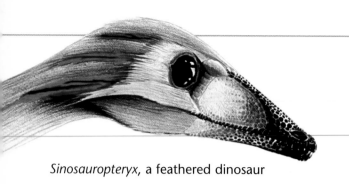

Sinosauropteryx, a feathered dinosaur

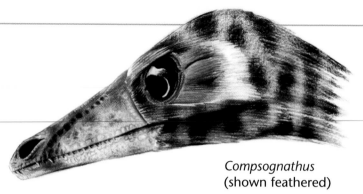

Compsognathus
(shown feathered)

When did the first feathers appear?

Many scientists view *Sinosauropteryx* as the most basal feathered dinosaur known. This means it has more primitive features than all other known feathered dinosaurs, including birds. But were these the earliest feathers? No. We know that *Archaeopteryx* and *Pedopenna* lived much earlier than *Sinosauropteryx* and had lots of feathers. The problem is that their feathers are quite advanced. This means that feathers had already been around for quite a while before the time of *Archaeopteryx*. So how can we figure out when the very first feathers appeared?

EVIDENCE: Another dinosaur, *Compsognathus*, gives us a clue as to what might be going on. *Compsognathus* was a small theropod that lived in the Jurassic period along with *Archaeopteryx* and *Pedopenna*. *Sinosauropteryx* is closely related to *Compsognathus*. If *Sinosauropteryx* had feathers, then why not *Compsognathus*? And if *Compsognathus* had feathers, then why not the common ancestor of *Compsognathus* and *Archaeopteryx* that lived in the Jurassic as well?

HYPOTHESIS: The common ancestor of *Compsognathus*, *Pedopenna*, and *Archaeopteryx* must have lived much earlier than any known feathered dinosaur, and therefore could have been the first to have feathers.

Dilophosaurus was a theropod more primitive than the group known to have feathers. How far back feathers really go, however, we do not know.

PROBLEM: Unfortunately this hypothesis does not really answer the question of when the first feathers appeared, though it does gives us an idea of how to look for them. It is possible that the first feathers appeared on theropods that lived even earlier than the common ancestor of *Compsognathus* and *Archaeopteryx*. These could be dinosaurs that have yet to be discovered. But perhaps well-known Jurassic theropods, such as *Allosaurus*, had feathers. Without more evidence, it's anyone's guess.

UNSOLVED MYSTERY!

What were the long feathers on *Caudipteryx* for?

When *Caudipteryx* and *Protarchaeopteryx* (see pp 12-13) were discovered, scientists were challenged to explain what two nonavian dinosaurs were doing with long feathers similar to those found on the tails of modern birds, including those that fly. They responded with two explanations.

EVIDENCE: *Caudipteryx* and *Protarchaeopteryx* had long symmetrical contour feathers on their arms and at the end of their tails.

HYPOTHESIS 1: These were simply feathers that had reached another evolutionary stage beyond hairlike structures. Although these contour feathers could not have been used for flight, they may have been useful for getting a little extra boost when jumping, for covering eggs in a nest, or perhaps for attracting mates.

HYPOTHESIS 2: While not supported as well as hypothesis 1, another possibility is that *Caudipteryx* and *Protarchaeopteryx* descended from dinosaurs that could fly. In this sense, they would have been similar to modern birds, such as penguins, that have lost the ability to fly.

Caudipteryx (right) was a turkey-size dinosaur that had long feathers on its arms and tail, but these feathers were not long enough for flight.

If *T. rex* had feathers at any stage of its life, it would have been as a baby, when feathers would have helped it stay warm or camouflaged. Here a young *T. rex* is shown in a nest near its parent.

Did *Tyrannosaurus rex* have feathers?

When *Sinosauropteryx* was found, scientists predicted that tyrannosaurs, such as *T. rex* and *Albertosaurus*, would be found to have had feathers as well. But until recently no tyrannosaurs had been found at Liaoning Province in China. And then came *Dilong paradoxus*.

EVIDENCE: In 2004 it was announced that a feathered tyrannosaur had been found in Liaoning Province. It was named *Dilong paradoxus*, meaning "puzzling imperial dragon." It was puzzling because, while its body had primitive features when compared to *T. rex* and other later tyrannosaurs, some features of its skull were fairly advanced. It was only about 6 feet (1.8 meters) long and lived almost 45 million years before the 45-foot-long (13.7 meter) giant *T. rex*. Several of *Dilong's* bones had fuzzy impressions, suggesting it was covered in shaggy hairlike feathers.

PROBLEM: It's one thing for a small dinosaur like *Dilong* to have feathers, but as animals get larger, the challenge shifts from staying warm to staying cool—unless, like woolly mammoths, they live in a cold environment. Lots of feathers would make it difficult for an animal as big as *T. rex* to stay cool. However, some very large prehistoric birds, such as the moa of New Zealand and the elephant bird of Madagascar, kept their feathers even as adults.

HYPOTHESIS: Tyrannosaurs, even large ones, had feathers when they were young and possibly kept them until they grew to the size of *Dilong* or the size of a moa. Once they reached that size, they probably lost their feathery coat in order to prevent overheating. Perhaps even medium-size tyrannosaurs had feathery coats.

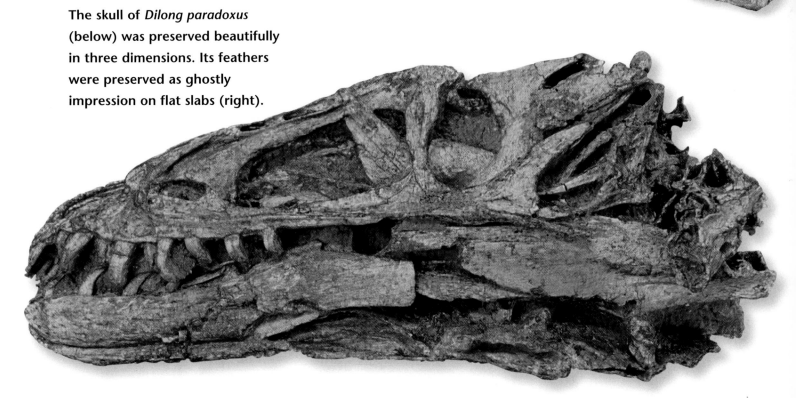

UNSOLVED MYSTERY!

And it is entirely possible that the largest tyrannosaurs kept feathers as adults for reasons other than keeping warm, just as birds do today. They might have had colorful feathers on their short arms and tails for mating displays or feathers near their ears, like owls, to improve hearing. Scattered filoplume feathers might have covered their bodies to sense vibrations. At this point, no one knows for sure.

The skull of *Dilong paradoxus* (below) was preserved beautifully in three dimensions. Its feathers were preserved as ghostly impression on flat slabs (right).

An artist used living dinosaurs—birds—as inspiration for the colorful coat shown here on a model of *Dilong*. At 6 feet (1.8 meters) long it is now one of the largest of the known feathered dinosaurs.

Is this dinosaur the closest relative of birds?

Sinornithosaurus milenii is a dromaeosaur that became well known for its birdlike body. Its name means "Chinese bird lizard of the millennium." It was so named because its discovery was announced in 1999, just before our calendars switched to 2000. Surrounding the dinosaur's body were areas with patches of downlike feathers. Its most remarkable features, however, were its overall proportions and its shoulder girdle.

EVIDENCE: In order to fly, a bird's arms must be almost as long as or longer than its legs. *Sinornithosaurus*'s arms were 80 percent the length of its legs, which is very close to bird proportions. Supporting these long arms in *Sinornithosaurus* was the most birdlike shoulder girdle known among nonavian dinosaurs. This shoulder girdle would have allowed *Sinornithosaurus* to flap its arms.

HYPOTHESIS: Some scientists suggest that if *Sinornithosaurus* had had flight feathers, it might have been a better flier than *Archaeopteryx*. But *Sinornithosaurus*, like *Sinosauropteryx*, was a living fossil with only a coat of hairlike feathers, living millions of years after the earliest birds. So it cannot be an ancestor of birds. Yet it may be similar in appearance to what dinosaurs looked like just before they took flight.

The fossil bones of *Sinornithosaurus* were lightweight and hollow, showing that this dinosaur was very closely related to birds.

HOW TO MAKE A DINOSAUR

Making a model of a dinosaur is a difficult business because dinosaur fossils provide only incomplete information about what the animals looked like in life. Bones are often missing, and there is usually no information at all about skin or any skin covering, such as feathers.

In the case of *Dilong*, scientists were lucky. The fossilized skeleton was fairly complete. It had a beautifully preserved skull and limb bones. Near several of its bones were impressions of long, downlike feathers, suggesting that they covered its body.

Dinosaur bones are often found in a heap, as was the case with *Dilong*. Through careful work, scientists sort out these bones one by one. They measure each bone with a precise ruler called a caliper (upper left).

To make a dinosaur, a carefully measured wire skeleton (left) is built to support clay. The dinosaur is then re-created muscle by muscle over the frame (right). Arms, teeth, and feathers are put on last.

Dinosaur bones are not often found perfectly laid out. *Dilong* was no exception. Its bones were preserved in a jumble that scientists had to sort out. And even though *Dilong* was well preserved, many of its bones were missing.

By looking at other closely related theropods, such as *Ornitholestes* and *Allosaurus*, as well as at other tyrannosaurs, a scientist and artist team can complete the skeleton of a dinosaur like *Dilong*. The artist can then take the skeleton and add muscle to it, based on his or her understanding of how similar muscles attach to bone in living animals, especially birds. Finally, feathers can be added to the model to match the length of those seen in the fossil. The color of eyes and feathers are not known from the fossil, so the artist again uses living birds as a guide.

The white bones in this illustration were all that was found of *Dilong.* An artist uses the fossils to set the length of the arms, legs, neck, and tail of the model. The inset shows a closeup of one of the tail bones. Notice the feathers.

DINOSAURS TAKE OFF

Of all the nonavian dinosaurs, only one, *Microraptor*, had wings suitable for taking to the air. Just how—and even if—it flew is still a matter of debate. Rather than making the answer to the question of how dinosaurs took flight more clear, this creature has scientists asking more questions. We can only hope that answers will be found by studying flight in living birds and through the discovery of new fossils from the period during which flight evolved—the Jurassic.

The only bird fossil known from the whole Jurassic period is *Archaeopteryx*, and the only known feathered nonavian dinosaur from the Jurassic is *Pedopenna*. There aren't many nonfeathered Jurassic dromaeosaurs or troodontids to study, either. Is this because these animals were rare in the Jurassic period? Probably not. This lack of evidence is more likely because fossil-bearing rocks of the right age are extremely rare on Earth. So scientists have to use the fossils they have, as well as evidence from living birds, to explain how dinosaurs took flight.

The best fossil clues come from *Archaeopteryx*, but *Archaeopteryx* was already a bird. What were even more primitive flying dinosaurs like—ones that were not yet birds? And what was the difference between them and the earliest birds? Those are the big questions in this chapter.

neornithine: The *neornithines* are the members of the group Neornithes, which includes living birds and all of their ancestors back to a common ancestor that lived millions of years ago. All neornithines have toothless beaks, clawless wings, and pygostyles instead of long bony tails.

airfoil: A thin surface, such as the wing of a bird or a bat, that interacts with air in such a way that it makes gliding or gliding possible.

pygostyle: The bony stump at the end of a bird's spine that serves as a base for tail feathers. It is all that remains of the long bony tails of early birds.

Words to Know

49

How did dinosaurs start flying?

Dinosaurs were certainly not the only creatures that ever took to the air. Flying evolved in vertebrates several times. Each time flying appeared, it happened in a different way, using different parts of the arm and hand. For example, bats evolved from small flightless mammals and fly with wings made of skin stretched between their fingers and legs. Pterosaurs, which evolved from a flightless archosaur, flew on wings of skin also, but their skin stretched from the tips of an extremely large and long finger all the way to their body.

Although the body parts used to create wings in bats, pterosaurs, and birds are different, they all produce the same result—a thin surface called an airfoil. Airfoils are necessary for gliding or para-chuting, which are both great ways of getting *down* safely from trees or other high places. The only way to get *up* to a high place

Nature experimented with flight many times, but always with an airfoil. Here, Cretaceous pterosaurs skillfully navigate the skies with their broad wings of skin and crests on their heads that may have served as steering devices.

without climbing, however, is to flap your airfoils and fly, unless you are attached to a jet engine or propeller. Flapping requires major changes to muscles and bones, such as those we see in dromaeosaurs, troodontids, and birds.

Archaeopteryx

But exactly how flight evolved in dinosaurs is a question that is the subject of much research and debate. Some of the questions being explored are: Why did dinosaurs start flapping? What good were long feathers to dinosaurs that lived on the ground? Did gliding from trees play any role in the evolution of flight?

EVIDENCE: Recent studies showed how both flapping and long feathers might have been useful for dinosaurs while they were still on the ground. One study showed that *Caudipteryx* and other nonavian feathered theropods could increase their running speeds by flapping their arms. Another study went further. One day the son of a scientist noticed at his father's laboratory that certain ground-dwelling birds could run up vertical walls. The birds did this by gathering speed and then flapping their small wings as they ran straight up. The father was intrigued and began to study this. What he learned was that flapping increased the bird's connection to the ground—or traction— and helped it run not only straight up, but sometimes even a little upside down. The more wing feathers a bird had— or the larger its airfoil—the better it could climb in this way. Both running faster and running up steep surfaces, such as trees, could have helped small dinosaurs to follow prey or escape from being eaten.

HYPOTHESIS: It is possible that flight began in dinosaurs as some combination of the ground-up and trees-down scenarios. For example, the first stage might have been arm and hand changes that made the evolution of the flight stroke possible in nonavian theropods. This might have been related to a food-gathering movement, such as snatching prey, made possible by the flexible wrists of maniraptors. Then small dinosaurs, already feathered for warmth and able to flap and climb, may have taken to the trees. From there, they could have become small tree-dwelling gliders. Details of these events have yet to be worked out.

UNSOLVED MYSTERY!

Did a four-winged dromaeosaur take to the air?

The announcement in 2003 of the discovery of a nonavian dinosaur with wings created a lot of excitement. Scientists hoped that such a creature might clarify how and when flight evolved. Instead *Microraptor gui* complicated matters. Why? Because the little dromaeosaur from China had long flight feathers on both its arms and its legs. In other words, it had four wings.

Until the discovery of *Microraptor*, there were no living or fossil examples of a creature with four feathery wings. One scientist, however, had proposed that such an animal might have existed. His name was William Beebe. In 1915, he wrote about a tetrapteryx, or four-winged, stage of bird evolution. He imagined an archosaur that climbed trees and then glided down using its broad airfoils.

Scientists who studied dinosaurs and the origins of flight knew what was required for two-winged flight. After all, living birds fly that way. Four-winged flight was a different matter and would require a new look into the role four wings might have played in the evolution of birds.

EVIDENCE: Specimens of *Microraptor* show long asymmetrical feathers on both its arms and its legs. Its tail shows a fan of feathers as well. *Microraptor*'s claws are sharply curved—a feature that helps tree-dwelling animals climb and hold onto branches. *Microraptor gui* and its close relative *Microraptor zhaoianus* are crow-size (not counting their long tails) and are the smallest known dromaeosaurs. This is important, since small, lightweight bodies are easier to get airborne than large, heavy ones.

HYPOTHESIS 1: An arboreal four-winged stage was important in the evolution of flight in birds.

HYPOTHESIS 2: *Microraptor* and other dromaeosaurs experimented with many body and feather variations as they became more birdlike on the ground. Among

Microraptor gui (artist's conception, left, and fossil, above) was a small dinosaur. Both its arm and leg feathers were asymmetrical, as can be seen in the close-up at right. The illustration at left shows the animal with its legs spread wide for gliding, something most dinosaurs could not do.

the experiments was this four-winged form with asymmetrical feathers. It may not have much to do with the evolution of flight in birds.

HYPOTHESIS 3: *Microraptor* and other flightless feathered dinosaurs, such as *Caudipteryx*, were not on their way to becoming more like birds at all. Instead, they were the descendants of birds that had lost or were losing the ability to fly.

PROBLEM: Theropod dinosaurs, including living birds, carry their legs directly under their bodies. The joint at their thighs does not allow for the hind legs to spread apart very far. How wide did *Microraptor* have to spread its leg wings to glide or parachute? How exactly did it use those leg wings? Scientists are conducting further studies to see how, or if, such flying or gliding could occur... and more fossils would help, too.

UNSOLVED MYSTERY!

What were early birds after *Archaeopteryx* like?

Birds that lived in the period immediately after *Archaeopteryx*'s time, known as the Cretaceous period, were plentiful and widespread. Fossils of early birds from this time are scattered on every continent, including Antarctica. From these fossils, scientists can begin to understand more about the origins of the only group of dinosaurs that is still living today—the neornithine birds.

EVIDENCE: The fossil remains of Cretaceous birds show that the change toward a form similar to living birds was rapid. Even some of the earliest birds had advanced traits. Their sharp teeth, like those seen on *Archaeopteryx*, disappeared and were replaced by beaks. Their long, bony tails shortened into pygostyles. Their sternums, or breastbones, got bigger quickly and became the place where large muscles for flapping wings attached. Their brains grew larger, too, which was a great advantage for navigating through the air and trees.

Yet not all early birds shared each of these advanced traits. There were many different "experiments" where the bodies of birds combined primitive

Boluochia zhengi was a thrush-size early bird from Liaoning Province in China. It had big claws on its feet, and although it still had teeth, its beak was hooked for tearing strips of meat from prey.

Rahonavis was a Late Cretaceous bird that lived in Madagascar. It had teeth, hand claws, a long tail and the slashing toe claws of a dromaeosaur.

and advanced traits. *Jeholornis*, an Early Cretaceous bird from Liaoning, had sharp teeth and a long tail supported by tiny rods, just like those found on dromaeosaurs. *Confuciusornis*, a bird that lived at Liaoning at the same time as *Jeholornis*, was just the opposite. Its beak was toothless and its tail was a stumpy pygostyle. *Rahonavis*, a bird from faraway Madagascar, displayed its dinosaurian ancestry with a large dromaeosaur-like claw on each inner toe. All of these birds kept their clawed fingers.

Early birds varied in size as well. Tiny *Iberomesornis* was a sparrow-size bird from Spain. In contrast, *Sapeornis* from China was twice as large as a crow. While *Iberomesornis* was flitting about in the undergrowth, *Sapeornis* may have been flying high and far. There were shorebirds and predators, too, such as *Boluochia*, which had a sharp beak at the tip of its toothed mouth. Some birds living in the Cretaceous even gave up their wings and became flightless diving birds, like the cormorants that live in the Galápagos Islands today. One flightless bird, called *Hesperornis*, lived in Russia and in the central area of North America, which during the Cretaceous was covered by a great sea.

HYPOTHESIS: Birds after *Archaeopteryx* took on many forms. All of these were spin-offs of the basic nonavian dinosaur form. In the end, the features that we see in living birds—toothless beaks, big brains, wings with no claws, pygostyles, and so forth—made up the only model that survived to modern times. All other forms of early birds were extinct by the end of the Cretaceous period.

Were some early birds good flyers?

Cretaceous birds, like modern birds, were of many kinds. Even if some early birds kept primitive features, this does not mean that they were poor flyers. In fact, the flight structures of some early Cretaceous birds are hard to tell from those of living birds. Here is an example of one early bird that flew just like some birds do today.

EVIDENCE: *Eoalulavis* was a Cretaceous bird with the earliest-known example of an alula (see below). The alula is used by birds to prevent stalling during slow flight by keeping the air that is flowing over the wing from becoming turbulent. Modern airplanes need this same kind of control for landing. They accomplish it with a slot that opens up on the front edge of the wing.

HYPOTHESIS: Among the early birds, there were some very good fliers. They had not only evolved lighter bodies and wings more suited to flying, but two of their three feathery dinosaurian fingers had fused together, leaving the third finger to shrink into one small thumblike wing: the alula.

It is interesting to find a structure useful for highly controlled flight, such as an alula, on *Eoalulavis*, a bird that lived in the early Cretaceous period. This suggests that birds were skillful fliers very soon after *Archaeopteryx*, a bird that did not have an alula.

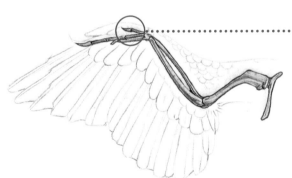

The earliest known example of an alula is found on *Eoalulavis* (right). The alula functions like a small extra wing that helps birds control their flight, particularly when they are trying to slow down.

Ratites, a group that includes ostriches and other ground-dwelling birds, is one of the oldest groups of neornithines. The common ancestor of living birds may have been a ground-dwelling bird as well.

When did modern birds appear?

There is debate about whether the common ancestor of neornithines lived before or after the great extinction at the end of the Cretaceous period 65 million years ago. There are fossil bits and pieces of birds from that period that some scientists identify as neornithine birds, but not all scientists agree that is what they are.

EVIDENCE: One recently studied fossil is *Vegavis iaai* from Antarctica. It was a bird closely related to ducks. If the scientists who studied it are correct, not only ducklike birds, but chicken and ratite (ostrich, kiwi, etc.) relatives lived before the end of the Cretaceous. Geneticists, scientists who study genes, have also presented evidence that neornithines lived before 65 million years ago. Their studies show that 22 major groups of neornithines survived the extinction event.

HYPOTHESIS: One common ancestor gave rise to all of the groups of birds living today. When it lived is uncertain, but based on fossil evidence we can say something about what it looked like. The most ancient of the neornithine groups are the flightless ratites, tinamous, ducks, and chickenlike birds. So the common ancestor of living birds was probably duck-size and lived primarily on the ground.

UNSOLVED MYSTERY!

58

WHEN IS A DINOSAUR A BIRD?

Now that we've reviewed the evidence that explains where birds came from, it should be easy to say what a bird is, right? Wrong. As more evidence pours in, things just get more complicated. Yet this is not a bad thing. It just means that there is still a lot of work for scientists interested in the origins of birds.

Still, scientists must draw a line somewhere on what is a bird and what is not. Most scientists accept *Archaeopteryx* as the most basal bird known. As they continue to study *Archaeopteryx,* they are finding just how slight the difference is between it and nonavian dinosaurs.

Archaeopteryx's bones look very much like those of a nonavian dinosaur. It had teeth, claws, and a long bony tail. Although it could fly, its body was not very well prepared for flight compared to other early birds.

Archaeopteryx's brain tells a different story, though. Scientists looked inside the bird's fossilized skull using a CT scanning machine that can create an image of what is inside stone. What they saw is that *Archaeopteryx*'s brain was like the brain of living birds. Even though this early bird did not yet have a body suited for powerful flying, its brain was ready to soar.

Aside from its feathers and large brain, the other major bird features of *Archaeopteryx* are shown below. Until evidence shows them otherwise, most scientists would agree that any dinosaur with these features is probably a bird.

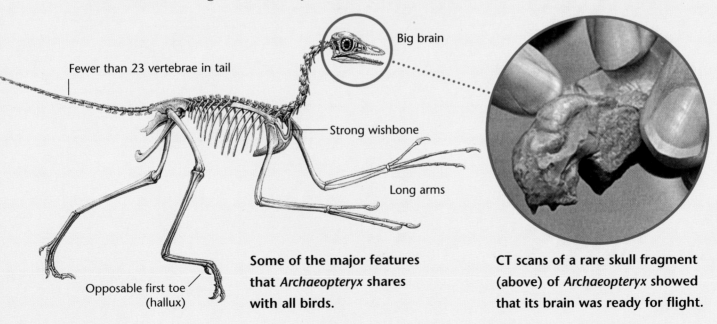

Fewer than 23 vertebrae in tail

Big brain

Strong wishbone

Long arms

Opposable first toe (hallux)

Some of the major features that *Archaeopteryx* shares with all birds.

CT scans of a rare skull fragment (above) of *Archaeopteryx* showed that its brain was ready for flight.

125-million year-old *Confuciusornis*, shown here as a mating pair, is a species long gone, but living birds surround us in such numbers that one could say that we still live in a dinosaur world.

THE END OF THE DINOSAURS?

There were lots of dinosaurs living 65 million years ago when something happened that wiped out much of the life on Earth. This event marked the end of the Mesozoic Era and the beginning of the era we are living in, the Cenozoic. The sudden disappearance of all the dinosaurs except neornithine birds at that time is remarkable. As far as we can tell, there were billions of ground-dwelling dinosaurs living on the planet at the time and even more billions of dinosaurs in the air. What could possibly have caused the death of so many animals?

One well-known suspect is a huge meteorite or asteroid that slammed into Earth near the Yucatan Peninsula in Mexico around 65 million years ago. But this alone does not completely explain the extinction of dinosaurs. The real answer is probably a combination of events or circumstances that has yet to be sorted out. As the answer becomes more clear, scientists will be better able to explain why birds survived and many plants and other animals did not.

UNSOLVED MYSTERY!

After the extinction event, the few neornithine birds that survived would have flown in lonely skies. The last of the flying pterosaurs had died out, and flying mammals, such as bats, had not yet evolved.

Dinosaurs, in the form of birds, have now risen again to become one of the most successful vertebrates on Earth. There are about 9,700 species and over 100 billion wild birds living today. Yet all is not rosy for them. Extinction looms again. One report suggests that as many as 1,300 species will disappear in the next 100 years and another 1,000 will be severely weakened. To compare, only 129 species went extinct in the last 500 years. This is bad for the birds, but it is also bad for Earth, since birds play an important role in ecosystems, as plant pollinators, seed dispersers, and scavengers, for example.

Extinction is a normal part of life—and death—on Earth, but the present rate of bird extinction is not normal. Humans are speeding up the process by destroying the habitats other creatures need to survive. So the next time you see a hummingbird, think of how lucky we are to have dinosaurs still among us, and try to think about what you can do to help keep them around for a long, long time.

Glossary

alula: A tuft of small feathers supported by the first digit, or "thumb," of a bird's hand.

archosaur: A group of reptiles, including dinosaurs, pterosaurs, and crocodiles. They first appeared at the end of the Permian period, about 248 million years ago.

avian: Relating to birds. The word comes from "Aves," the group that contains all living and fossil birds.

bipedal: Walking or moving using only two legs.

coracoid: The bone of the shoulder girdle that connects to the scapula to form the shoulder joint. The coracoid may also connect with the sternum and furcula.

Cretaceous period: The last period of the Mesozoic Era. It lasted from approximately 145 million years ago to 65 million years ago and ended with a great extinction.

Dinosauria: The group that contains dinosaurs and their descendants. The word is Greek for "fearfully great lizards," but is more commonly translated as "terrible lizards."

dromaeosaur: A group of birdlike theropods that includes *Velociraptor* and *Deinonychus*. They are best known for having a large claw on their second toe and tails strengthened by rods.

furcula: The "wishbone" of a dinosaur or bird. It is formed by the fusion of the two collarbones.

hallux: In birds and theropods, the hallux is a reduced first toe. In most birds, it is rotated and allows the foot to grasp a perch or prey.

Jurassic period: The middle period of the Mesozoic Era that lasted from approximately 205 million years ago to 145 million years ago.

maniraptorans: A theropod group known for their long arms and unique wrist bone. The group includes dromaeosaurs, troodontids, and birds.

Ornithischia: One of two major divisions of dinosaurs, defined by their "birdlike" hips. Birds are not closely related to ornithischians, which include horned dinosaurs and duck-billed dinosaurs, among others.

oviraptorids: A group of theropods known for their beak-shaped, toothless jaws.

pterosaur: Extinct flying reptiles with wings of skin that stretched between the body and long fourth finger.

pygostyle: A set of fused vertebrae that occur at the end of a bird's tail. The pygostyle supports tail feathers.

Saurischia: One of two major divisions of dinosaurs, defined by their "lizardlike" hips. The group includes theropods and sauropods.

sauropod: A major group of four-legged, long-necked dinosaurs. Some were the largest known land animals.

scapula: The shoulder blade.

shoulder girdle: A set of bones that includes the scapula, coracoid, and furcula. Together these bones form a structure critical for flight in birds.

sternum: A bone in the center of the chest that in birds has been enlarged to support strong muscles.

therizinosaurs: A group of long-necked theropods known for their long hand claws and small teeth.

theropod: A member of a large group of meat-eating dinosaurs that includes tyrannosaurs, oviraptorids, dromaeosaurs, troodontids, therizinosaurs, and birds, among others.

troodontids: Small, long-legged maniraptorans with large brains and retractable claws on their second toe.

Triassic period: The first period of the Mesozoic Era. It lasted from approximately 250 million to 205 million years ago.

Alan Groves perches among his dinosaur creations at his studio in Australia. All of the sculptures that appear in this book are his work.

Index

Bibliography

I am not a dinosaur scientist, but like you, I *love* dinosaurs. And I *love* dinosaur artwork. I've brought these two passions together in this book, which I hope you will find a fascinating exploration into the dinosaurian ancestry of birds. If there's one thing you bring away, I hope it is a new appreciation for the process of science. As you probably noticed, scientists do not know all the answers to everything, but they do follow a method. By reviewing evidence and making hypotheses, they eventually arrive step by step at explanations that match the evidence. These explanations may be days, weeks, or even years away, but they will come. In the meantime, if you would like to learn more about this subject, I recommend the following resources:

Books:
Chiappe, Luis M., and Lawrence M. Witmer. *Mesozoic Birds.* University of California Press, Berkeley and Los Angeles, 2002.
Currie, Philip J., et al, eds. *Feathered Dragons.* Indiana University Press, Bloomington, 2004.
Barrett, Paul. National Geographic *Dinosaurs.* National Geographic Society, Washington, DC, 2001.
Paul, Gregory. *Dinosaurs of the Air.* Johns Hopkins University Press, Baltimore, MD, 2002.
Paul, Gregory, ed. *The Scientific American Book of Dinosaurs.* St. Martin's Press, New York, 2000.
Sloan, Christopher. *Feathered Dinosaurs.* National Geographic Society, Washington, DC, 2000.

Magazine Articles:
Ackerman, Jennifer. "Dinosaurs Take Wing." *National Geographic,* July 1998.
Norell, Mark. "The Proof Is in the Plumage." *Natural History,* July-August 2001.
Sloan, Christopher. "Feathers for T. rex." *National Geographic,* November 1999.

Websites:
The Museum of Paleontology
    http://www.ucmp.berkeley.edu/
National Geographic Society Dinorama
    http://www.nationalgeographic.com
    /dinorama/

Credits

Cover: Alan Groves. Back cover, page 1: John Sibbick. 2-3: Alan Groves. 3: Lizard, Chris Sloan. 4: John Sibbick. 5: Map, Chris Sloan. Photo, Xu Xing. 6: Tim Laman. 7: Jaime Headden. 8: From Owen (1879: pl. 47). 9: Lou Mazzatenta. 10: John Sibbick. 11: Alan Groves. 12-13: Portia Sloan. 14: Xu Xing. 15: Jaime Headden. 16: Brian Cooley, Ira Block. 16-17: Portia Sloan. 18: Top, Mick Ellison. Bottom, Tim Laman. 19: John Sibbick. 20-21: Portia Sloan. 22: Mick Ellison. 23: Jaime Headden. 24: Xu Xing. 25: Top, Portia Sloan. Bottom, Hope Ryan. 26-27: Alan Groves. 28: Lou Mazzatenta. 29: Top, Warren Jacobs. Bottom, Lou Mazzatenta. 30: Top, Mick Ellison. Bottom, Portia Sloan. 31: Mick Ellison. 32: Chris Sloan. 33: Rob Clark. 34-35: Chris Sloan. 36: Lou Mazzatenta. 37: Jaime Headden. 38: Top, Jaime Headden. Bottom, Richard Nowitz. 39: Lou Mazzatenta. 40: Michael Skrepnick. 41: Xu Xing. 42-44: Alan Groves. 45: Lou Mazzatenta. 46: Xu Xing. 47: Top, Alan Groves. Bottom: Xu Xing. 48: John Sibbick. 49: Jaime Headden. 50: John Sibbick. 51: Jaime Headden. 52: Portia Sloan. 53: Xu Xing. 54-55: Xioa-lian Zeng, courtesy of Xu Xing, IVPP. 56: Jaime Headden. 57: Left, Portia Sloan. Right, Lou Mazzatenta. 58: Des and Jen Bartlett. 59: Left, John Sibbick. Right, courtesy of www.DigiMorph.org. 60: Xiao-lian Zeng & Jin-feng Hou, courtesy of Xu Xing, IVPP. 62: Alan Groves.

One of the world's largest nonprofit scientific and educational organizations, the National Geographic Society was founded in 1888 "for the increase and diffusion of geographic knowledge." Fulfilling this mission, the Society educates and inspires millions every day through its magazines, books, television programs, videos, maps and atlases, research grants, the National Geographic Bee, teacher workshops, and innovative classroom materials. The Society is supported through membership dues, charitable gifts, and income from the sale of its educational products. This support is vital to National Geographic's mission to increase global understanding and promote conservation of our planet through exploration, research, and education.

For more information, please call 1-800-NGS LINE (647-5463) or write to the following address:

National Geographic Society
1145 17th Street N.W.
Washington, D.C. 20036-4688 U.S.A.

Visit the Society's Web site at www.nationalgeographic.com.